an introduction to

chain indexing

PROGRAMMED TEXTS IN
LIBRARY AND INFORMATION SCIENCE
SERIES EDITOR C D BATTY BA FLA

An introduction to colon classification
by C D Batty

An introduction to the Dewey decimal classification
by C D Batty

An introduction to Sears list of subject headings
by Philip Corrigan

An introduction to UDC
by Jean M Perreault

Learn to use books and libraries
by T W Burrell

T D WILSON

an introduction to

chain indexing

CLIVE BINGLEY  LONDON

FIRST PUBLISHED 1971 BY CLIVE BINGLEY LTD
16 PEMBRIDGE ROAD LONDON W11
SET IN 10 ON 12 POINT LINOTYPE PLANTIN
AND PRINTED IN THE UK BY
THE CENTRAL PRESS (ABERDEEN) LTD
COPYRIGHT © T D WILSON 1971
ALL RIGHTS RESERVED
0 85157 109 3

CONTENTS

FOREWORD
by Dr S R Ranganathan

Determining the subject heading of a book is an important piece of work in cataloguing. When I learnt cataloguing in the University College, London, in 1924, much attention was not paid to this. In a few classes we were asked to guess the subject heading. In the course of the year, I found that there was some guidance in the *Rules for dictionary catalogue*, by C A Cutter. But the application of these rules required judgement of an involved nature. When I began to teach cataloguing in the Madras University in 1929, I found that the students did not feel sufficiently enlightened by this method of fixing the subject heading. Therefore, I introduced them to the use of the American Library Association's *List of subject headings*. Two difficulties were felt by the students in the use of this *List*. One was that for a new subject not represented in the *List*, it was not easy for them to construct the subject heading. Secondly, the abler students felt no challenge in this method; they felt bored.

By 1935, I realised that the determination of the subject heading was in essence equivalent to the determination of the class number. This made me examine whether the work already done in assigning class number cannot also serve in assigning subject heading. I examined the *List* from this angle. But there was no explicit clue given in that book as to how the committee arrived at their several subject headings. This made me find out how they might have arrived at them. After some trial, it struck me that the headings in the *List* were closely correlated to decimal class numbers. Then I tried to work out the nature of the correlation. This was the genesis of 'chain procedure', now named 'chain indexing'. I applied this method with the colon class number also as the basis. I found that in a few cases where a heading in the *List* did not agree with the decimal chain, it agreed with the colon chain. This made me infer that:

1 The committee on subject headings was more sensitive to the readers' approach than the decimal class number;

2 The colon class number was as sensitive to the readers' approach as the committee was.

This made me feel that a secondary use of chain procedure might well be a means of comparing two different schemes for classification.

I incorporated the idea and the method of chain indexing in my *Theory of library catalogue* (1938). The rules of my classified catalogue code for subject heading were reframed on the basis of chain indexing in its second edition (1945). But I had brought the chain indexing method into use even in 1936, both in the catalogue of the

8

Madras University Library and in teaching cataloguing in that university. I found that the cataloguer felt a considerable saving of time by the use of this method and that it also gave satisfaction to the students, in fact I found them enjoying this method of establishing subject headings. It is gratifying to learn that chain indexing has become the commonly accepted method today, as Mr Wilson puts it.

During the last thirty years the chain indexing method has been continuously refined to meet the requirements of micro subjects. This process of refinement has opened up an apparently never-ending line of research for cataloguers. This in itself is a great merit of chain indexing. Many interesting results of research in chain indexing are coming up almost every year in the Annual Seminar of the Documentation Research and Training Centre (Bangalore). These concern the advanced cataloguing of micro documents.

When I began teaching in 1917, I soon realised the necessity for replacing the mass-lecturing method of teaching by the method of individual instruction. I was then teaching mathematics. I found that it gave a very good return to the satisfaction of myself and that of the students. I, therefore, adopted this method in teaching library science also. I have been continuing it all these years. I am glad that this method of individual instruction is coming into vogue in the schools of library science in the UK. It puts the students ever in the active mood of search through personal effort. This is the best way of helping each student to educate himself to his own fullness, along his own lines, and at his own speed. Now a tendency has begun to print and publish the ' notes of lessons ' suited to this method. For the first time, I heard the expression ' scrambled textbook ' to denote this kind of notes of lessons in the books of Mr C D Batty relating to the teaching of classification by decimal classification and colon classification respectively.

Mr Wilson has now brought out a scrambled textbook on teaching chain indexing. First I wondered why he asked me to write this introductory note to his book. Further correspondence showed me that he was a student in the school of library science at Newcastle when I conducted a few lessons there in 1956. This fact has added a personal charm to the opportunity given to me to write these few words as a foreword to Mr Wilson's excellent *Introduction to chain indexing: a programmed textbook.*

S R RANGANATHAN

PREFACE

This programmed text is intended as an elementary introduction to a subject which is often a source of considerable difficulty for students. For this reason I have emphasized the most fundamental aspects of the technique: for more advanced methods and problems the student is referred to the brief bibliography.

The text has been tested with groups of students and when used as a class text it has been found that the best method is to use it as a supplement to normal lectures, that is, giving additional examples and exercises as students complete a specific problem area dealt with in the text.

I would like to acknowledge here the assistance I have received from my colleagues in the Department of Librarianship, particularly Mr G A Ibbs who field-tested the text. I am also grateful to the editor of this series, Mr David Batty, for his helpful criticisms of the original draft, and to Mr Derek Austin of BNB who made some last-minute suggestions, and I am especially indebted to Dr S R Ranganathan who made many useful suggestions and who wrote the foreword. Needless to say, for any errors and eccentricities that remain I am wholly responsible.

I also feel that due recognition ought to be given to the work of

A J Wells and his colleagues at BNB who pioneered the technique in our national bibliography, and did it so effectively as to create what is in effect a ' national authority file ', consulted whenever practical problems arise.

Those parts of the book directly reproduced from the 17th edition of the *Dewey decimal classification*, and from the *British national bibliography* are by permission of the copyright owners.

Finally, I would like to acknowledge a major debt by dedicating this book to my mother and to the memory of my father: without their self-sacrifices my professional career, and hence this book, would have been impossible.

T D WILSON
BSC (ECON), FLA
Principal lecturer
Department of Librarianship
Newcastle upon Tyne Polytechnic

INSTRUCTIONS

This is a ' scrambled ' or ' programmed ' textbook. It is based on the knowledge that different individuals progress at different speeds in learning and allows them to go at their own pace, rather than having to ' run with the pack ' in a lecture.

The classification scheme used in the examples in this book is the 17th edition of the Dewey *Decimal classification* (DC), and you will need a copy of the schedules by you as you work through the book.

Read each piece of instruction carefully and choose an answer from those given at the end of the section, or do the piece of practical work set. Then turn to the frame indicated by the answer and proceed as before.

Above all don't be disheartened by making mistakes—that's how we learn.

Now turn to frame 1 and begin.

Frame 1

One of the chief types of library catalogue is that in which the major section contains main entries arranged in classified order by the notational symbols of the classification scheme in use in the library.

This kind of catalogue is called:

A dictionary catalogue—frame 2

A classified catalogue—frame 3

An alphabetico/classed catalogue—frame 4

Frame 2

No, you have made the wrong choice.

A *dictionary catalogue* consists of a single alphabetical sequence of names of subjects, names of authors, and first words of titles.

If you are uncertain of the distinctions between different types of catalogues you should read the appropriate chapters of a general text-book such as A C Foskett's *Subject approach to information* (Bingley, 1969), or the definitions in T Landau's *Encyclopedia of librarianship* (Bowes, 1961).

Now go back to frame 1 and choose the correct name.

Frame 3

Yes, this is the correct answer.

The kind of catalogue used by the majority of British libraries is the *classified catalogue*. It has three parts: the classified section that gives it its name, an alphabetical subject index, and an author/title section. The section of the catalogue with which this text is concerned is the alphabetical subject index, which is intended as a guide to:

The classified section of the catalogue—frame 5

The shelves—frame 6

The author/title section—frame 7

Frame 4

No, you have made the wrong choice.

An *alphabetico/classed catalogue* is arranged by the names of subjects *not* by notational symbols. The names are grouped first into broad subject categories, and within these successively into finer subject divisions.

If you are uncertain of the distinctions between different types of catalogues you should read the appropriate chapters of a general text-book such as A C Foskett's *Subject approach to information* (Bingley, 1969), or the definitions of T Landau's *Encyclopedia of librarianship* (Bowes, 1961).

Now go back to frame 1 and choose the correct name.

Frame 5

Good, you have chosen the correct answer.

Although the alphabetical subject index can act as a guide to the shelving arrangement, its principal purpose is to guide the user to the classified section of the catalogue. Because the classified section arranges entries according to a systematic grouping of subjects perhaps unfamiliar to the user, and because the subjects are represented by symbols from an artificial notation, the user needs a guide from the name of the subject in natural language to its place in the classified section. Here he will find entries for all books possessed by the library, rather than only those which happen to be on the library shelves.

You have grasped the basic idea of an alphabetical subject index and it is now necessary to study its relationship to the classified section more closely.

Turn to frame 8 for further information.

Frame 6

You are only partly correct.

It is true that the alphabetical subject index can act as a guide to the shelves but this is not its main function. Not all the stock of a library will be on the shelves—some material will be on loan, some away being bound, and so on. The purpose of the index is to act as a guide to the subject order of the entire stock as found in the classified sequence.

Now go back to frame 3 and choose the correct answer.

Frame 7

No, you have made the wrong choice.

Although title entries in the author/title index may be guides to the subject content of books to a certain extent, the alphabetical subject index cannot possibly guide the user to them, since it refers to the notational symbols of the classification scheme.

Now go back to frame 3 and choose the correct answer.

Frame 8

The intention of the alphabetical subject index is to complement the classified section, *ie* it has to do a job which that section cannot do, namely, bring together in an alphabetical sequence those topics which the classification scheme separates; *eg,* in the classified section the following topics will be separated—

BRITISH PUBLIC LIBRARIES	027.442
BRITISH POLITICAL PARTIES	329.942
ECONOMIC HISTORY OF GB	330.942
A HISTORY OF THE BRITISH ISLES	942

Thus various aspects of British culture are separated by the structure of the scheme.

The alphabetical subject index brings these topics together in the following manner:

GREAT BRITAIN : ECONOMIC HISTORY	330.942
GREAT BRITAIN : HISTORY	942
GREAT BRITAIN : POLITICAL PARTIES	329.942
GREAT BRITAIN : PUBLIC LIBRARIES	027.442

In defining the alphabetical subject index, therefore, we can say:

It contains entries for the subject of books—frame 9

It complements the classified section by drawing together the distributed relatives—frame 10

It guides the user to the correct class number for a subject—frame 11

Frame 9

The answer you have chosen is only partly true.

Note that the index entries are not entries as found in a catalogue, *ie* they give no description of the book, but simply a subject term (or group of terms) and the appropriate class number.

The point made by the previous section was that the alphabetical subject index performs a job which the classified sequence cannot do—namely, that of bringing together under the name of the subject the aspects of that subject which are scattered by the structure of the classification scheme.

If you now understand this point turn to frame 10; if not, return to and re-read frame 8 and then turn to frame 10.

Frame 10

Good, this is absolutely correct.

Now we must consider how the alphabetical subject index is constructed. One commonly accepted method today is known as *chain indexing*, so called because the method uses the concept of a chain of classes from the main class to the subdivision under which the book is classified. Thus, in any one main class we have as many chains as there are subdivisions, *eg*, in 800 LITERATURE we have:

800   LITERATURE
810   AMERICAN LITERATURE
813   AMERICAN FICTION
813.5 20TH CENTURY AMERICAN FICTION

or

800   LITERATURE
820   ENGLISH LITERATURE
821   ENGLISH POETRY
821.8 ENGLISH POETRY OF THE VICTORIAN PERIOD

Using the schedules of DC, now write down the chain of the class number: 214.8.

To check your answer turn to frame 12.

Frame 11

You are partly correct.

The alphabetical subject index does act as a guide to the correct class number for a subject, but the point made by the previous lesson was that it performed a job which the classified sequence could not do— namely that of drawing together under the name of a subject the aspects of that subject which are scattered by the structure of the classification scheme.

If you now understand this point turn to frame 10; if not, return to and re-read frame 8 and then turn to frame 10.

Frame 12

The correct chain is:

200	RELIGION
210	NATURAL RELIGION
214	THEODICY
214.8	PROVIDENCE

If your own answer does not agree with this check carefully to find out where you went wrong.

Now try: 336.274, and turn to frame 13 for the answer.

Frame 13

The correct chain is:

300	THE SOCIAL SCIENCES
330	ECONOMICS
336	PUBLIC FINANCE
336.2	TAXATION (COMPULSORY REVENUES)
336.27	OTHER TAXES
336.274	LICENCES

Again, check your answer and then try this more difficult class number: 837.910 8.

Turn to frame 14 for the answer.

Frame 14

The correct chain is:

800	LITERATURE
830	LITERATURE OF GERMANIC LANGUAGES
837	GERMAN SATIRE
837.91	20TH CENTURY GERMAN SATIRE
837.910 8	COLLECTIONS OF 20TH CENTURY GERMAN SATIRE

If you have arrived at some other answer it is possibly because you have had difficulty in following the 'divide-like' notes in the literature class. Check very carefully and make sure that you understand the instructions.

Now turn to frame 15 and continue the course.

Frame 15

You will now know what a *chain* of classes is.

The next step is to understand what we mean by *analysing the chain*. In this process we must identify the specific subject of each digit in the class number under which the document is classified. To do this it is useful to write the chain of classes down in a different form.

A moment ago we used the example 813.5 20TH CENTURY AMERICAN FICTION; its chain was:

800   LITERATURE

810   AMERICAN LITERATURE

813   AMERICAN FICTION

813.5   20TH CENTURY AMERICAN FICTION

We can analyse the chain thus

8

  1

    3

     .5

and then identify the meaning of each digit by writing alongside it the specific meaning of that digit, *ie* that aspect of the total subject which that digit identifies, thus:

8   LITERATURE

  1   AMERICAN

    3   FICTION

     .5 20TH CENTURY

Now do the same thing for 821.8 and turn to frame 16 for the answer.

Frame 16

The correct analysis is:

    8   LITERATURE
    2   ENGLISH
    I   POETRY
     .8   VICTORIAN PERIOD

Analysing the class number in this fashion is an essential step—*it must be done on every occasion,* otherwise links in the chain will be missed.

Now turn to frame 17.

Frame 17

The importance of analysing the chain may not be recognised without a little further comment. Chain indexing is a near-automatic procedure; how automatic depends upon the classification scheme used. In a perfectly designed scheme chain-indexing would be perfectly automatic, but this would depend upon the careful analysis of every class number. Hence, for a scheme which is less than perfect, the analysis of the chain is an *absolute essential.* If you try to do chain indexing without analysing the chain you will fail dismally—it must be done on every occasion. Having established what a chain is and the importance of analysing it, we have to consider how to use this information in constructing the subject index entries.

Now turn to frame 18.

Frame 18

In constructing *subject index* entries a number of rules must be followed.

The first of these is:

Rule 1: the first term to be indexed is that which identifies the last link in the chain.

In the case of the class number 841.009 where 9 means CRITICISM, what will be the first term to be listed for entry in the index?

Check your answer in frame 19.

Frame 19

The correct answer is CRITICISM, this being the last term in the chain. If you did not choose this term re-read Rule 1 in frame 18 and check your analysis again.

Now try again with the following numbers:

616.931 5

725.87

581.55

Turn to frame 20 for the answers.

Frame 20

The correct terms are:

616.931 5 BOTULISM
725.87 BOATHOUSES
581.55 COMMUNITIES

In order to complete the first index entry it is usually necessary to identify the context of the first term, *eg,* in the index to the 17th edition of the decimal classification scheme BOTULISM appears in seven different contexts, BOATHOUSES in two and COMMUNITIES in eight. For this reason the next rule is necessary:

Rule 2: each index entry should consist of the term for the link, plus one or more subheadings qualifying the term where it is necessary to define the subject more clearly. The index entry is then completed by the addition of the class number appropriate to the link.

Now select the most appropriate term for the statement below:

It is necessary to provide subheadings for index terms in order to remove .... (REDUNDANCY, AMBIGUITY, DUPLICA-TION).

Turn to frame 21.

Frame 21

The correct answer is:

'It is necessary to provide subheadings for index terms in order to remove AMBIGUITY.' If a concept is associated with more than one subject field, the user of the catalogue must be enabled to locate that aspect which is of interest to him; thus if he found an index entry:

COMMUNITIES 581.55

he would not be pleased to find information on botanical aspects if he was interested in human society.

Bearing Rule 2 and the above points in mind, is the following statement true or false?

The first index entry for the class number 837 does not require the use of subheadings.

TRUE—frame 22
FALSE—frame 23

Frame 22

No—you have chosen the wrong answer.

The first index entry for the class number 837 would be under the term SATIRE and, since this concept appears in all literature, its context must be specified.

Return to frame 21 and resume the course from the statement of Rule 2.

Frame 23

Good, you have chosen correctly.

Of course SATIRE, which is the first term to be indexed, must be qualified, because it is a concept which may occur in any literature. Having established the need for qualification of terms by the use of subheadings in order to remove ambiguity from index entries, we must now establish a rule which tells us which subheadings to use:

Rule 3: the subheadings intended to define the first term in an entry should be chosen from the chain in strict order of increasing generality.

Now analyse the following number: 841.009. Turn to frame 24.

Frame 24

The correct analysis is:

8	LITERATURE
4	FRENCH
1	POETRY
.0	(meaningless digit)
0	(meaningless digit)
9	CRITICISM

In accordance with Rule 1 the first term to be indexed is CRITICISM and according to Rule 2 we must qualify it by using subheadings. Now, according to Rule 3 which terms should be used as subheadings?

CRITICISM: FRENCH LITERATURE	841.009—frame 25
CRITICISM: POETRY	841.009—frame 26
CRITICISM: POETRY: FRENCH LITERATURE	841.009—frame 27
CRITICISM: POETRY: LITERATURE	841.009—frame 28

Frame 25

No, you have not made the correct choice.

This class number does not refer to a book on criticism of French literature as a whole, but only to criticism of one literary form within that literature.

Remember Rule 2: ' each index entry should consist of the term for the link, plus one or more subheadings qualifying the term where it is necessary to define the subject more clearly '.

Thus the index entry should include the terms for the literary form, and for the language in which the literature is written, *ie* the correct entry is:

CRITICISM: POETRY: FRENCH LITERATURE   841.009

Note that the qualifying subheadings POETRY and FRENCH LITERATURE are used in the index entry in order of their appearance in the *ascending* chain.

Now turn to frame 27 and resume the course.

Frame 26

No, you have made the wrong choice.

This class number does not refer to the criticism of poetry in general, but to the criticism of that form within French literature.

Remember Rule 2: 'each index entry should consist of the term for the link, plus one or more subheadings qualifying the term where it is necessary to define the subject more clearly'.

Thus the index entry should include the terms for the literary form *and* for the language in which the literature is written, *ie* the correct entry is:

CRITICISM: POETRY: FRENCH LITERATURE 841.009

Note that the qualifying subheadings POETRY and FRENCH LITERATURE are used in the index entry in order of their appearance in the *ascending* chain.

Now turn to frame 27 and resume the course.

Frame 27

Good, the correct index entry would be:

CRITICISM: POETRY: FRENCH LITERATURE 841.009

Note that CRITICISM: POETRY is not sufficient because it does not completely remove ambiguity; it is necessary to use further subheadings to accomplish this. Note also that the qualifying subheadings POETRY and FRENCH LITERATURE are used in the index entry in order of their appearance in the *ascending* chain.

The final rule is:

Rule 4: entries are made for every sought link in the chain back to the basic subject.

In the case of the class number 841.009 we had analysed the chain as

8	LITERATURE
4	FRENCH
I	POETRY
.o	(meaningless digit)
o	(meaningless digit)
9	CRITICISM

How many entries are to be made altogether, and what terms are they for?

Check your answer in frame 29.

Frame 28

No, you have made the wrong choice.

This class number does not refer to the criticism of poetry in general but to the criticism of that form within French literature.

Remember Rule 2: 'each index entry should consist of the term for the link, plus one or more subheadings qualifying the terms where it is necessary to define the subject more clearly'.

Thus the index entry should include the terms for the literary form and for the language in which the literature is written, *ie* the correct entry should be:

CRITICISM: POETRY: FRENCH LITERATURE 841.009

Note that the qualifying subheadings POETRY and FRENCH LITERATURE are used in the index entry in order of their appearance in the *ascending* chain.

Now turn to frame 27 and resume the course.

Frame 29

Your answers should be: four—CRITICISM; POETRY; FRENCH LITERA-
TURE and LITERATURE.

Each of these four terms is a link in the chain of classes and must,
therefore, be accounted for in the indexing process.

Now let us look at a complete example making use of all four rules.
The subject to be indexed is represented by the class number 821.
First we analyse the number:

8   LITERATURE

  2   ENGLISH

   1 POETRY

and the index entries according to the rules will be:

Rule 1: POETRY

Rules 2 and 3: POETRY: ENGLISH LITERATURE 821

Rule 4: ENGLISH LITERATURE 820

       LITERATURE 800

Note that we have no entries for:

ENGLISH POETRY, or LITERATURE, ENGLISH

Why not?

Because no one would look for them—frame 30

Because such entries would duplicate the job done by the classified
sequence of the catalogue—frame 31

Because they offend against Rule 4—frame 32

Frame 30

No; it is quite possible that someone may search for these terms—but, when making a subject index, consideration must be given to the economics of doing so and to the functions performed by other parts of the catalogue.

If we make entries in the subject index such as:

LITERATURE 800

LITERATURE, ENGLISH 820

LITERATURE, FRENCH 840

LITERATURE, GERMAN 830

this section will correspond very closely to the hierarchical sequence of the classified part of the catalogue, *ie* the entries would duplicate the job done by the classified sequence. Remember that the alphabetical subject index must *complement* the classified sequence, *not* duplicate it.

Now turn to frame 29 and choose the correct answer.

Frame 31

Good, this is correct.

It is uneconomic to provide entries in an alphabetical subject index which duplicate the structure of the classified part of the catalogue. If we made entries for all possible combinations of terms the index would be much too bulky and expensive to make. Consider for example, the subject we have been dealing with:

POETRY: ENGLISH LITERATURE 821

If all combinations of the three words in this entry were put into the alphabetical subject index we would have (in addition to the entry above) the following:

POETRY: LITERATURE, ENGLISH   821
ENGLISH LITERATURE: POETRY   821
ENGLISH POETRY: LITERATURE   821
LITERATURE: POETRY, ENGLISH   **821**
LITERATURE: ENGLISH POETRY   821

ie a total of six entries for the one class number. We restrict our entries, therefore, to those which do not duplicate the job already done by the classified sequence. Thus, if a user does search for ENGLISH POETRY he will find the entry

ENGLISH LITERATURE 820

and the arrangement and guide cards of the classified sequence will lead him to the appropriate subdivision.

You should now be able to do a set of entries for a simple number: first, analyse the following class number:

343.1

To check turn to frame 33.

Frame 32

Yes, it is true that such entries would offend against Rule 4, but the question is—why do we have this rule? The answer to this lies in the economics of making an alphabetical subject index. If we make an entry:

LITERATURE, ENGLISH

this is simply translating the class number digit by digit:

8   LITERATURE

820 ENGLISH

and thus we are putting into the index entries which express the hierarchy of the classification scheme in the same manner as the notation. In other words the alphabetical subject index would simply duplicate the job already being done by the classified file.

If you are still unsure on this point return to frame 8 and review the course from there; if you can now choose the correct answer return to frame 29 and do so.

Frame 33

The correct answer is:

3   SOCIAL SCIENCES

4   LAW

3   CRIMINAL LAW

.1 PROCEDURE, TRIALS, EVIDENCE

Now, assuming that the work classified here is called FAMOUS CRIMINAL TRIALS what will be the first index entry we make according to Rules 1, 2 and 3?

TRIALS: LAW: SOCIAL SCIENCES 343.1—frame 34

CRIMINAL TRIALS: LAW 343.1—frame 35

EVIDENCE: LAW 343.1—frame 36

TRIALS: CRIMINAL LAW 343.1—frame 37

Frame 34

No, you are wrong.

Trials are a feature of different kinds of law: criminal, civil, military and canon. The subheadings used must indicate the exact content of the term TRIALS. Now choose the correct answer:

CRIMINAL TRIALS: LAW 343.1—frame 35

TRIALS: CRIMINAL LAW 343.1—frame 37

Frame 35

No, you have made the wrong choice.

Remember, those terms are chosen which indicate the meaning of a specific digit in the class number. In this case three terms are provided for the digit .1 PROCEDURE, TRIALS AND EVIDENCE. Your task (at this stage) is to select the most appropriate term as the first index entry and then decide which terms should be used as subheadings.

Return to frame 33 and try again.

Frame 36

No, you have chosen the wrong answer.

You are right to choose only one term from those given for the final link, but you have chosen the wrong one—the book is concerned with FAMOUS CRIMINAL TRIALS—try again.

TRIALS: LAW: SOCIAL SCIENCES 343.1—frame 34

CRIMINAL TRIALS: LAW 343.1—frame 35

TRIALS: CRIMINAL LAW 343.1—frame 37

Frame 37

Good, this is correct.

It is not necessary to add any subheadings because the term TRIALS is now given its exact context by the subheading CRIMINAL LAW. To add LAW would be merely to duplicate a term, and it is not necessary to add SOCIAL SCIENCES because this is the chief location of law, and other kinds of law can be indicated by appropriate subheadings giving their correct context.

The remaining steps in the analysis are:

3   SOCIAL SCIENCES

4   LAW

3   CRIMINAL LAW

Applying all the rules once again, which will be the next index entry?

LAW, CRIMINAL: SOCIAL SCIENCES 343—frame 38

CRIMINAL LAW 343—frame 39

LAW: SOCIAL SCIENCES 343—frame 40

Frame 38

No, you have obviously not been paying attention to the text.

Remember that you must choose the terms *as given*: with a simple subject like this there is no necessity to begin inventing your own entries. Effectively what you are trying to do is to enter under the term LAW—quite rightly, *but not at this stage*. The number you are indexing is 343 and specifically, the final digit.

Return to frame 37 and choose the correct term.

Frame 39

CRIMINAL LAW is the correct index entry.

This now leaves us with

3 SOCIAL SCIENCES

 4 LAW

Which of the following is the final set of index entries?

1) LAW: SOCIAL SCIENCES 340

    SOCIAL SCIENCES 300—frame 41

2) LAW 340

    SOCIAL SCIENCES 300—frame 42

3) LAW 340—frame 43

Frame 40

No—you have missed a step.

Perhaps you think that because CRIMINAL LAW has appeared as a subheading there is no necessity to use it on its own. But in that event how will someone who wishes to find information on the subject locate the entries in the file?

Return to frame 37 and choose the correct entry.

Frame 41

There is certainly nothing wrong with this set of entries.

However, it is not usually necessary to add the main class term when the chief location of a subject is in that class, and when the risk of ambiguity is therefore slight. Normally, therefore, one would omit the subheading from LAW: SOCIAL SCIENCES.

Now turn to frame 44 to continue the course, which will proceed to examine some of the problem areas of chain indexing.

Frame 42

Quite correct.

It is unnecessary to qualify the term LAW with the subheading SOCIAL SCIENCES because most aspects of law are in this class; the exceptions can be qualified as appropriate.

We are now ready to examine some of the problems of chain indexing, because, unfortunately, not everything is quite as straightforward as the examples already given.

Turn to frame 44.

Frame 43

You are partially correct.

There must, of course, be an entry for LAW but, because of the habit of catalogue users of looking under broader concepts than that in which they are truly interested, it is advisable to index also the more general term SOCIAL SCIENCES.

Now turn to frame 44 and continue the course, which will examine some of the problem areas of chain indexing.

Frame 44

The first problem to be tackled is that of *compound headings*.

This is something which has already been dealt with in the CRIMINAL TRIALS example without further comment. A compound heading is one which covers more than one concept, as in

343.1 PROCEDURE, TRIALS, EVIDENCE

The rule for entering such headings is that only the term relating specifically to the book in hand must be indexed.

A compound heading may occur in the form given above, or in the form of two concepts joined by ' and ', *eg,*

312.5 (Statistics on) MARRIAGE AND DIVORCE

or in the form of an inclusion note, *eg,*

271.1 BENEDICTINES including CELESTINES, CLUNIACS

Which of the following numbers is accompanied by a compound heading?

341.57 —frame 45
248.3 —frame 46
370.195—frame 47

Frame 45

No. 341.57 does not have a compound heading, it is a compound *term, ie,* the name of a single concept formed by more than one word. A compound heading is one which covers more than one concept. Try again:

248.3 —frame 46
370.195—frame 47

2*

Frame 46

Good. You have learnt how to identify a compound heading.

The rule for compound headings, as mentioned earlier, is that only the term appropriate to the book in hand is indexed. In the case of a book about STATISTICS OF DIVORCE, class number 312.5, the analysis would reveal the chain:

3	SOCIAL SCIENCES
1	STATISTICAL METHODS AND STATISTICS
2	STATISTICS OF POPULATIONS
.5	ON MARRIAGE AND DIVORCE

Which of the following will be the correct first index entry?

DIVORCE: STATISTICS 312.5—frame 48

STATISTICS OF DIVORCE 312.5—frame 49

MARRIAGE AND DIVORCE STATISTICS 312.5—frame 50

Frame 47

No. 370.195 does not have a compound heading.

A compound heading is one which covers more than one concept. COMPARATIVE EDUCATION is the name of a single concept formed from two words.

Return to frame 44 and try again.

Frame 48

Good, you have evidently remembered the earlier rules correctly.

We can now move on to the remaining problems, beginning with *hidden links*. A hidden link is one which does not have a specific class number. In earlier editions of the decimal classification scheme these were often missed altogether, but in the 17th edition they have been made obvious by printing them in their correct generic positions and indicating their presence through the use of a solid marginal arrow.

Which of the following are hidden links?

312	STATISTICS OF POPULATION (DEMOGRAPHY)—frame 51	
331.3	SPECIFIC AGE GROUPS—frame 52	
335.1-335.3	UTOPIAN AND HUMANITARIAN SYSTEMS—frame 53	
494	URAL-ALTAIC, PALEOSIBERIAN, DRAVIDIAN LANGUAGES—frame 54	

Frame 49

Oh dear! You have forgotten the earlier rules: the specific term denoted by the 5 of 312.5 in relation to this document is DIVORCE.

STATISTICS is the next most general class and therefore can be used as a subheading.

Now return to frame 46 and choose the correct answer.

Frame 50

Oh no! This is a very silly answer.

Remember that if a number of terms is given for a link you must choose only that term which is descriptive of the subject of the document. We are concerned only with statistics of DIVORCE.

Now return to frame 46 and choose the *correct* answer.

Frame 51

No. Remember that a hidden link is centred on the page and indicated by a marginal arrow. 312 is not such a heading. A further guide is that hidden links are usually represented by a block of numbers rather than a single number.

Return to frame 48 and choose the correct answer.

Frame 52

Wrong.

SPECIFIC AGE GROUPS has an individual class number and is not *hidden*—and if you look again you will see that there is no marginal arrow.

Now return to frame 48 and choose the correct answer.

Frame 53

Quite correct.

This example has the hallmarks of a *hidden link*:

(a) there is a block of numbers;

(b) there is a marginal arrow.

Note that what we are doing is returning to the subject of analysing the chain. Simple chains are easy to analyse, but in DC many chains are far from simple, and they embody problems which we are now trying to clarify.

Now we come to the question of how to deal with these hidden links. The answer is quite straightforward—we must include them in our initial analysis of the class number and decide which ones we need subject index entries for.

Examine the following number and analyse it, indicating all hidden links:

347.5

Turn to frame 55 for the correct answer.

Frame 54

No. Many single numbers in DC cover a group of topics—this does not make them hidden links. What you are looking for is a group of topics or a single topic without a single specific number. Now return to frame 48 and choose the correct answer.

Frame 55

The complete analysis of 347.5 is (hidden links are given in parentheses):

3	SOCIAL SCIENCES
4	LAW
(342-349)	(MUNICIPAL, INTERNAL LAW)
7	PRIVATE LAW AND JUDICIAL SYSTEM
(347.1-347.8)	(PRIVATE LAW)
.5	TORT, NEGLIGENCE, DAMAGE

If your analysis does not exactly duplicate that above, check to see what you have missed. The most likely step to be missed is:

(342-349) MUNICIPAL (INTERNAL) LAW.

Note that 347.5 is subordinate to this class.

Now try: 526.32.

Turn to frame 56 for the correct analysis.

Frame 56

The correct analysis is:

526.32	BENCH MARKS
526.3	GEODETIC SURVEY
(526.1-526.7	GEODESY)
526	MATHEMATICAL GEOGRAPHY
520	ASTRONOMY AND ALLIED SCIENCES

Again, if your analysis is wrong, check to find out why.

In this last chain we have two examples of our next problem—the *false link*. Note again that the problems which occur are problems of analysis; we are now going to cover earlier ground in greater depth. This serves to emphasise the importance of analysis in making the actual indexing as automatic as possible.

Now turn to frame 57 for further information on *false links*.

Frame 57

False links may take a number of different forms.

Firstly, a false link may be one which does not represent a concept. This is termed a *redundant digit*. In DC the zero is usually a false link, since it is used either to make up the three-figure minimum, as in 320 POLITICAL SCIENCE, or to introduce standard subdivisions, *eg*, 620.00212 SPECIFICATIONS.

Which of the following numbers contain a redundant-digit type of false link?

403
370.193 4
352.006

Turn to frame 58 for the answer.

Frame 58

The correct answer is that all three numbers include redundant digits and, therefore, false links.

A second type of false link is one which represents a time concept which lacks a proper name, as in the standard subdivisions -0901/09046.

Which of the following numbers contain this type of false link?

620.1891—frame 59
589.225 —frame 60
354.420009034—frame 61

Frame 59
No.

This number includes a redundant digit type of false link, not a time concept; the subject is simply MERCURY.

Return to frame 58 and try again.

Frame 60

No.

This number represents UREDINALES and includes no false links at all.

Return to frame 58 and try again.

Frame 61

Good. You have chosen correctly.

This number, which means GOVERNMENT OF BRITAIN FROM 1800 TO 1900, includes both the redundant digit and the time concept type of false link.

The third and final type of false link is one which represents a class which is not strictly superordinate to one below—*eg,* 600 TECHNOLOGY is not properly superordinate to 610 MEDICAL SCIENCE. This is probably the most difficult type of false link to identify, because it requires some knowledge of the interrelationships between subjects.

Which of the following numbers has a chain which includes this last type of false link?

574.55 —frame 62
645.1 —frame 63
793.732—frame 64

Frame 62

No.

The chain for 574.55 is:

574.55 COMMUNITIES
574.5 ECOLOGY
574 BIOLOGY
570 BIOLOGICAL SCIENCES
500 SCIENCE

This is a perfectly acceptable chain.
Return to frame 61 and try again.

Frame 63

Yes, you have chosen correctly.

The class number 645.1 has the following chain:

645.1 FLOOR COVERINGS
645 HOUSEHOLD FURNISHINGS
640 DOMESTIC ARTS AND SCIENCES
600 TECHNOLOGY

DOMESTIC SCIENCE or HOME ECONOMICS would be more fittingly regarded as a basic class, and therefore the link to 600 is a false link. Note that 793.732 also includes a false link—CROSSWORD PUZZLES are hardly regarded as among the ARTS. Here RECREATIONS is the basic class.

Which of the following numbers includes false links of *any* type?

623.8432—frame 66
701.17　—frame 70
925　　—frame 72

Frame 64

Good. You are correct.

The chain for 793.732 is:

793.732	CROSSWORD PUZZLES
793.73	PUZZLES
793.7	GAMES NOT CHARACTERISED BY ACTION
793	INDOOR GAMES
790	RECREATION
700	THE ARTS

Here, 790 RECREATION can be regarded as the basic class. The link to 700 is false, because RECREATION is not an art in the normal sense of the latter word. Note also that 645.1 includes a false link from DOMESTIC SCIENCE to TECHNOLOGY.

Which of the following numbers includes false links of *any* type?

623.8432—frame 66

701.17 —frame 70

925 —frame 72

Frame 65

The correct chain index entries are:

SCIENTISTS : BIOGRAPHY 925

BIOGRAPHY 920

The next major problem in chain indexing is the *unsought link,* which is defined as one representing a concept for which readers are unlikely to search when looking for the specific subject represented by the final digit of the class number. An example may help to explain this:

331.62	IMMIGRANTS
331.6	OTHER GROUPS
331.3-331.6	SPECIAL CLASSES OF WORKERS
331	LABOUR
330	ECONOMICS

OTHER GROUPS and SPECIAL CLASSES OF WORKERS are vague terms which are unlikely to be sought.

What, therefore, would be the correct chain index entries?

Turn to frame 67 for the answer.

Frame 66

Wrong. 623.8432 does not have a false link in its chain.

You may have thought that it had because it is subordinate to 620—but the zero does not occur in the actual class number. Such numbers are best analysed thus:

623 MILITARY AND NAVAL ENGINEERING

62 ENGINEERING

6 TECHNOLOGY

Return to frame 63 or 64 and try again.

Frame 67

The correct chain index entries are:

IMMIGRANTS : LABOUR ECONOMICS 331.62

LABOUR ECONOMICS 331

ECONOMICS 330

Note that LABOUR and ECONOMICS can be run together to form a phrase which is generally accepted in the world of economics. Note also that although 331.3-331.6 is a *hidden link,* it is also *unsought,* and is therefore not included. Thus, some of our initial analysis may seem wasted, but it must nevertheless be done scrupulously on every occasion, lest important steps otherwise be missed.

Obviously the idea of an unsought link is open to personal interpretation in many instances, but if common sense is applied a reasonable decision can be reached.

Analyse the following number completely:

364.135

Turn to frame 71 for the answer (but not before you have done it yourself).

Frame 68

The correct index entries are:

PIRACY: CRIMINOLOGY 364.135

OFFENCES: CRIMINOLOGY 364.1

CRIMINOLOGY 364

Note that OFFENCES is not included in the first index entry. The reason for this is that to do so would simply be repetitious, since it adds nothing to the definition of PIRACY which CRIMINOLOGY does not.

Another problem is present in the class number 526.32 MATHE-MATICAL GEOGRAPHY. 526 is obviously a subdivision of GEOGRAPHY, but that superordinate term does not appear in the chain. What do we do?

a) Forget about it—frame 69

b) Put in another entry reading GEOGRAPHY—frame 73

c) Invert the heading to GEOGRAPHY, MATHEMATICAL—frame 75

Frame 69

No. To forget it would no doubt be the easiest way out, but would hardly assist the reader who wanted to know where all aspects of geography were to be found. We must, therefore, provide an entry which will file next to GEOGRAPHY, but show where its MATHEMATICAL aspects are to be found.

Return to frame 68 and choose the correct answer.

Frame 70

Right—701.17 includes the obvious false link—the zero which is used to introduce the standard subdivisions. You should also have noticed that 925 includes a false link—turn to frame 72 to find out why.

Frame 71

The correct analysis is:

364.135	PIRACY
364.13	AGAINST CONSTITUTED AUTHORITY (unsought link)
364.13-.17	SPECIFIC KINDS OF OFFENCES (unsought link)
364.1	OFFENCES
364	CRIMINOLOGY
36	WELFARE AND ASSOCIATIONS (false link)
3	SOCIAL SCIENCES

Now, leaving out the unsought and false links, what will the correct index entries be?

Turn to frame 68 for the answer.

Frame 72

Good. 925 includes a false link. If we analyse the number, we get:

925 SCIENTISTS

92 BIOGRAPHY

9 GENERAL GEOGRAPHY AND HISTORY AND RELATED DISCIPLINES

ie, 900 is a 'hold-all' class which includes a number of subjects, and to add its name to BIOGRAPHY in a chain index entry would be superfluous. You should also have noticed that 701.17 includes a zero which is a redundant digit type of false link discussed in frame 59—*ie,* it does not represent a concept, but is used to introduce standard subdivisions.

What would the chain index entries for the number 925 be?

Turn to frame 65 for the correct answer.

Frame 73

If you were to do this, what class number would you put beside it?

You could hardly put GEOGRAPHY 526, because this number covers only MATHEMATICAL GEOGRAPHY. You need an entry which will file next to GEOGRAPHY, but which will indicate that only the MATHEMATICAL aspects are to be found at 526. There is, therefore, only one kind of entry which will suffice, and that is the inverted heading:

GEOGRAPHY, MATHEMATICAL 526

Now turn to frame 75.

Frame 74

No. The chain for 617.3 is:

617.3 ORTHOPEDIC SURGERY

617 SURGERY

610 MEDICINE

Thus, since SURGERY appears in the chain, there is no need to invert the heading ORTHOPEDIC SURGERY.

Return to frame 75 and try again.

Frame 75

Good—this is correct.

You may be wondering why the heading

GEOGRAPHY, MATHEMATICAL 526

is allowed, when earlier in the program headings such as LITERATURE, ENGLISH were expressly forbidden. The answer is quite simple: in the case of the number 820 ENGLISH LITERATURE there is a superordinate class LITERATURE in the same chain. In the case of 526, the superordinate class GEOGRAPHY is missing, because this aspect of geography is separated from other aspects, and to invert the heading is the neatest solution to the problem. Now, in order to test you on this, say whether the following class numbers include links for which inverted headings must be used:

617.3 —frame 74

330.91—frame 76

574.5 —frame 77

Frame 76

Good. 330.91 does present a problem, because its heading reads:

ECONOMIC GEOGRAPHY

and it is separated from general aspects of GEOGRAPHY at 910; thus, in addition to the normal-order heading ECONOMIC GEOGRAPHY, the inverted heading GEOGRAPHY, ECONOMIC will be needed.

Now we cheated a little on this number, because you will observe that the correct notation for ECONOMIC GEOGRAPHY is not a single number, but a block of numbers, 330.91-330.99, and, therefore, the index entries will take the form:

ECONOMIC GEOGRAPHY 330.91/330.99

and

GEOGRAPHY, ECONOMIC 330.91/330.99

This block of numbers has a note which reads:

Add area notations 1-9 to 330.9

Which of the following numbers will be the correct one for ECONOMIC GEOGRAPHY OF PICARDY?

330.9-426 —frame 78
330.9426 —frame 81
330.94426 —frame 82

Frame 77

No. 574.5 has a perfectly normal chain:

574.5   ECOLOGY
574   BIOLOGY
57   ANTHROPOLOGICAL AND BIOLOGICAL SCIENCES
5   SCIENCE

So there is no heading to be inverted.
Re-read frame 78 and then choose the correct answer.

Frame 78

No, you have chosen the wrong number.

The hyphen is not used as a notational symbol in the decimal classification scheme, and is dropped when the area number is transferred to a class number.

Now return to frame 76 and try again.

Frame 79

You have obviously forgotten how to analyse a class number.
  When this is done correctly, the result is as follows:

4	EUROPE
4	FRANCE
2	NORTHERN FRANCE
6	PICARDY

The correct answer to the previous question, therefore, is ' 6 '.
Now turn to frame 84.

Frame 80

No, you are wrong.
  Remember that if you perform the analysis correctly, each digit should represent a specific concept, in this case as follows:

4	FRANCE
2	NORTHERN FRANCE
6	PICARDY

The correct answer to the previous question, therefore, is ' 6 '.
Now turn to frame 84.

Frame 81

This is careless!

You must add to a class number the entire block of numbers following the hyphen.

Now return to frame 76 and choose the correct answer.

Frame 82

Good. The correct number is 330.94426.

Now, in this number, which digit (or group of digits) represents PICARDY?

4426—frame 79
426 —frame 80
26 —frame 83
6 —frame 84

Frame 83

You have not performed the analysis of the class number correctly.

Remember that in a class number, each digit usually represents a specific concept, and in this case ' 2 ' represents NORTHERN FRANCE, and only ' 6 ' represents PICARDY.

Now turn to frame 84.

Frame 84

Good. The correct answer is that only the final digit ' 6 ' represents PICARDY.

This exercise is designed to show that any digits which you add as a result of following an ' add area notations ' instruction must be analysed in the same way as any other set of digits. In the case of the area tables, the situation is made a little more complex, because unsought links and hidden links tend to be rather more numerous than in other parts of the tables, and therefore even greater care is necessary.

Having achieved a correct analysis, do we now:

a) Index only the final digit and enter it in the index as:
   PICARDY: ECONOMIC GEOGRAPHY 330.94426?—frame 88

or

b) Index as many steps in the geographical chain as necessary?
   —frame 90

Frame 85

If this is what you insist upon doing, then go ahead—but one day you will run out of catalogue drawers, and will have to find an alternative. The correct answer is that we use a general reference card with the following type of entry:

DICTIONARIES

Dictionaries on specific subjects are shelved with the subject. The subject number has 03 added to it to identify a dictionary—*eg,*
books on ELECTRONIC ENGINEERING—621.381
dictionaries of ELECTRONIC ENGINEERING—621.38103

The more specific the catalogue's instructions to the user, the more easily will he find the information he requires.

What would be the first index entry given to a DIRECTORY OF THE PLASTICS INDUSTRY 688.4025?—frame 91

Frame 86

Good. This is a sensible solution; otherwise, the catalogues would in time become full to bursting point. The general reference would take the following form:

DICTIONARIES

Dictionaries on specific subjects are shelved with the subject. The subject number has 03 added to it to identify a dictionary—*eg,*
books on ELECTRONIC ENGINEERING—621.381
dictionaries of ELECTRONIC ENGINEERING—621.38103

The more specific the catalogue's instructions to the user, the more easily will he find the information he requires.

What would be the first index entry given to a DIRECTORY OF THE PLASTICS INDUSTRY 668.4025?—frame 91

Frame 87

The correct answer is:

FRANCE: ECONOMIC GEOGRAPHY 330.944

and the subsequent entries will be:

EUROPE: ECONOMIC GEOGRAPHY 330.94

ECONOMIC GEOGRAPHY 330.9

The standard subdivisions, also usually introduced by means of 'divide-like' notes, require special treatment. Imagine what the subject index would look like if every time a subject dictionary was catalogued, we added a new card; there would be dozens of entries under 'dictionary', and the same for other subdivisions. What then do we do?

a) Put in a new card regardless of how many subject dictionaries we have—frame 85

b) Put in a general reference card drawing attention to the notation of a dictionary—frame 86

c) Forget all about it and turn to something else—frame 89.

Frame 88

No, this is the wrong answer.

You must give at least the same consideration to each link in a geographic chain as you would give to any other part of a chain.

Now turn to frame 90.

Frame 89

Don't despair at this late stage—we are almost at the end of the course.
Return to frame 87 and try again!

Frame 90

Good. One must treat geographic subdivisions like any other subdivisions, and index any links which are likely to be sought links. In
this instance there is one unsought link. Which is it?

4	EUROPE	—frame 92
4	FRANCE	—frame 93
2	NORTHERN FRANCE	—frame 94
6	PICARDY	—frame 95

Frame 91

Answer: a general reference of the form:

DIRECTORIES
> Directories of specific subjects are shelved with the subject. The subject number has 025 added to it to identify a directory—*eg*, books on PLASTICS—668.4
> DIRECTORY OF THE PLASTICS INDUSTRY—668.4025

Of course such entries are only given once—the next directory to be added to stock would be indexed under subject, and the form element in the class number would be ignored.

Now turn to frame 96.

Frame 92

No. Remember the definition (frame 65) of an unsought link: 'one which represents a concept for which readers are unlikely to search'.

Surely EUROPE must be a term which people are likely to search for in this example.

Return to frame 90 and try again.

Frame 93

No. Surely someone interested in PICARDY is likely to think that, since Picardy is part of France, he should search under FRANCE in the index? The definition of an unsought link given in frame 65 is ' one which represents a concept for which readers are unlikely to search '.

Return to frame 90 and try again.

Frame 94

Good. This is the right answer.

It is unlikely that anyone will require all aspects of NORTHERN. Compass points are usually regarded as unsought terms. We have already noted in frame 84 that

PICARDY : ECONOMIC GEOGRAPHY

will be the first index entry. What will be the next?

Turn to frame 87.

Frame 95

Surely not!

The specific subject of the book is THE ECONOMIC GEOGRAPHY OF PICARDY. What better term, therefore, for a first entry than PICARDY?

Return to frame 90 and try again.

Frame 96

Chain indexing is designed to enable users to locate books by subject. There is, however, a difficulty in that the class number for a book may be greater in extension than the subject of the book itself—*ie* it may be impossible to classify as specifically as is desirable. Chain indexing provides the answer to this problem through the device of *verbal extension* of the class number. For example, if we have a book on MUDRA, the symbolic emblems and gestures used in Buddhist meditation practices, the nearest we can get in DC is:

294.3437 SYMBOLISM, SYMBOLIC OBJECTS, EMBLEMS

When analysing this number, however, we should extend the class number thus:

294.3437 MUDRA

294.3437 SYMBOLISM

BNB used the [1] notation to extend the class number, and this is useful since it provides notational extension as well as verbal extension. A suitable first index entry, therefore would be:

MUDRA: SYMBOLISM: BUDDHISM 294.3437 [1]

An example from technology is:

URANIUM FUELS FOR NUCLEAR REACTORS

Closest class number: 621.48335 FUELS

Index entry: URANIUM: FUELS: NUCLEAR REACTORS 621.48335 [1]

If you have a book entitled PROGRAMMING DIGITAL COMPUTERS, the closest class number for which is 621.381958, what would be the first index entry?

Turn to frame 98.

Frame 97

Answer:

DIGITAL COMPUTERS   621.381958

COMPUTERS: ELECTRONIC ENGINEERING   621.38195

ELECTRONIC ENGINEERING   621.381

ENGINEERING   620

Now turn to frame 99 for information on how to deal with synonyms.

Frame 98

The answer is:

PROGRAMMING: DIGITAL COMPUTERS   621.381958 [1]

What would the remaining index entries be?

Turn to frame 97 to discover.

3*

Frame 99

Synonyms do not present a serious problem in a chain index, because the indexer simply makes entries for all synonyms as he comes across them. Typical examples are found in the life sciences, where things have both scientific and common names—*eg*,

584.25   IRIDACEAE (IRIS)

This would be given two entries in the alphabetical subject index :

IRIS : FLOWERING PLANTS : BOTANY   584.25

IRIDACEAE : FLOWERING PLANTS : BOTANY   584.25

Note, however, that the indexer must always be alert to detect synonyms himself. What would be the synonym for the subject at 297?

Turn to frame 100.

Frame 100

The answer is MOHAMMEDANISM.

This term is now regarded as rather archaic, but it is still found from time to time, and may be searched for no less than ISLAM. Index entries would be required for each term.

Now try indexing 616.953 completely, remembering to do the analysis first.

Turn to frame 101.

Frame 101

The correct analysis is:

616.953	RABIES (HYDROPHOBIA)
616.95	VENEREAL AND ZOOGENOUS DISEASES
616.91—616.96	COMMUNICABLE DISEASES (hidden link)
616.9	OTHER DISEASES (unsought link)
616.1 —616.9	SPECIFIC DISEASES (hidden link)
616	MEDICINE
610	MEDICAL SCIENCE
600	TECHNOLOGY (false link)

What will the correct index entries be?

Turn to frame 102.

Frame 102

The required index entries are:

RABIES: DISEASES: MEDICINE   616.953

HYDROPHOBIA: DISEASES: MEDICINE   616.953

These are the required synonymous terms given in the schedules.

ZOOGENOUS DISEASES: MEDICINE   616.95

ANIMAL-BORNE DISEASES: MEDICINE   616.95

Again, these are synonymous terms. ZOOGENOUS DISEASES is the correct term to choose from the compound heading.

COMMUNICABLE DISEASES: MEDICINE   616.91/616.96

CONTAGIOUS DISEASES: MEDICINE   616.91/616.96

More synonyms!

DISEASES: MEDICINE   616.1/616.9

Note that SPECIFIC is not a sought term.

MEDICINE   616

MEDICAL SCIENCES   610

If you have got this completely correct, then you have done very well.

Now turn to frame 103.

Frame 103

We have concentrated in this text on the alphabetical subject index, but it must be remembered that this is linked to the classified file, which must be adequately guided to ensure that the user can find the items for which he is searching. The usual means of achieving this is by the use of guide cards, but these can be augmented by *feature headings*. A feature heading consists of the last term in the chain, which is added to the class number at the beginning of the entry in the classified file, thus:

621.381958   DIGITAL COMPUTERS
LEVEY, Mark
    An introduction to computers for the layman . . .

BNB uses feature headings extensively, and some examples from the bibliography may clarify the concept.

Turn to frame 104.

Frame 104

Examples from BNB of the use of feature headings:

633—Crops

633.4—Root crops

633.49—Tubers

633.491—Potatoes

633.491[1]—Diseases

    MI-DOX early warning manual for

      diseases and pests of potatoes . . .

678—Rubber

678.6—Natural rubber

678.64—Properties

678.64[1]—Testing. *Specifications.*

    BRITISH STANDARDS INSTITUTION

      Methods of testing vulcanized rubber . . .

739.2—Work in precious metals

739.23—Silver

739.23[1]—Hallmarks.

    BLY, John

      Discovering hallmarks on English silver . . .

Note that in a card catalogue only the final feature heading would actually appear on the card for the actual document.

Now turn to frame 105.

Frame 105

It must also be realised that it is necessary to keep some control over the headings adopted for class numbers, in order to ensure consistency. This is done by maintaining an *authority file,* which consists of a file of class numbers in schedule order, together with the heading or headings adopted—*eg,*

581.128   ANAEROBIC RESPIRATION : PHYSIOLOGY : BOTANY

581.129   TRANSPIRATION : BOTANY

581.13   NUTRITION : PHYSIOLOGY : BOTANY

581.13   METABOLISM : PHYSIOLOGY : BOTANY

581.132   DIGESTION : PHYSIOLOGY : BOTANY

What would the authority file entries be for the following class numbers?

391.44

391.5

Turn to frame 106.

Frame 106

The authority file entries would be :

391.44   FANS : COSTUME

391.44   PARASOLS : COSTUME

391.44   CANES : COSTUME

391.44   EYEGLASSES : COSTUME

391.5   HAIRSTYLES : FASHION

391.5   BEARDS : FASHION

391.5   WIGS : FASHION

Note the change in terminology for the subheading, necessitated by an inadequate degree of subdivision in the classification scheme.

Turn to frame 107.

Frame 107

We have now come to the end of the text. Naturally, in concentrating upon fundamentals we have left a good deal unsaid: chain indexing is relatively automatic but not completely so, and much must be left to the indexer to discover in the course of practical work. Many of the problems that occur cannot be formalised very easily and, hence, depend for their solution upon the flair of the indexer. But with this text as a basis, the indexer should be better placed to exercise that flair.

APPENDIX I

1 Television in the school. Class no: 371.335 8
  Analysis:
  a) 371.335 8 —Television
  b) 371.335   —Visual materials and devices
  c) 371.33   —Audio-visual materials for teaching
  d) 371.3   —Methods of instruction and study
  e) 371   —The school
  f) 37   —Education
  g) 3   —Social sciences

Comment: some of the above terms should be amended before use, eg link d) to the more familiar 'Teaching methods', b) to 'Visual aids', and c) to 'Audio-visual aids'. Link e) is, in this context, unsought, and 'Education' is a sufficiently basic class to index back to.

Index entries:
Television: Visual aids: Education—371.335 8
Visual aids: Education—371.335
Audio-visual aids: Education—371.33
Teaching methods: Education—371.3
Education—370

2 The peregrine. Class no: 598.9
  Analysis:
  a) 598.9[1]   —Peregrine
  b) 598.9   —Falconiformes (Birds of prey)
  c) 598.3-.9   —Specific orders
  d) 598.2   —Aves (Birds)
  e) 598   —Reptiles and birds
  f) 592-599   —Taxonomic zoology
  g) 590   —Zoological sciences

Comment: link a) is a verbal extension, b) should have 'Birds of prey' modified to 'Predators', c) is a hidden, but unsought, link, e) is a false link, f) should be modified to Taxonomy, and g) to Zoology.

Index entries:
  Peregrine: Birds—598.9[1]
  Predators: Birds—598.9
  Falconiformes: Birds—598.9
  Birds: Zoology—598.2

Aves: Zoology—598.2
Taxonomy: Zoology—592-599
Zoology—590
Note that synonyms are indexed directly to the class number—there are no specific references in a chain index file.

3 Fashion drawing. Class no: 741.672
Analysis:
a) 741.672 —Fashion drawing
b) 741.67 —Advertisements and posters
c) 741.64-.69 —For specific mediums
d) 741.6 —Illustration (Commercial art)
e) 741.5-.7 —Drawing and drawings for specific purposes
f) 741-744 —Drawing and drawings
g) 74 —Drawing and decorative arts
h) 7 —The arts
Comment: work it out for yourself from the entries given below.
Index entries:
Fashion drawing: Commercial art—741.672
Commercial art—741.6
Drawing—741/744
Arts—700
Fine arts—700

4 Archaeological excavation. Class no: 913.031 028 3
Analysis:
a) 913.031 028 3—Excavation of remains
b) 913.031 028 —Techniques
c) 913.031 —Archaeology
d) 913.03 —Man and his civilization
e) 913 —Geography of ancient world
f) 913-919 —Geography of specific continents . . .
g) 910 —General geography
h) 900 —General geography and history . . .
Comment: work it out for yourself again.
Index entries:
Excavation: Archaeology—913.031 028 3
Archaeology—913.031

APPENDIX II

Fill in the missing word/s or tick the correct item as appropriate.

1 Chain indexing is a method of alphabetical .... indexing.

2 An index based on chain indexing is a guide to the .... part of the classified catalogue.

3 For the class number 214.8 the first term to be indexed will be ....?

4 Index entries are made for every .... link in a class number.

5 Index headings require .... to define the subject clearly.

6 Subheadings must be chosen in strict order of increasing ....

7 Chain indexing economises in the number of index entries allotted to a book because it does not duplicate the structure of the ....

8 Which of the following headings are not allowed under the rules of chain indexing? a) Literature; b) Literature, French; c) Criticism; d) English poetry; e) English literature.

9 A heading which covers more than one concept is called a .... heading.

10 341.57—Commercial law is/is not a heading which covers more than one concept.

11 When indexing a class number which covers more than one concept one chooses:

a) the full class name as given in the heading

b) only the term relating to the book in hand.

12 The indicator for a hidden link in DC is a ....

13 A link which represents a time concept without a proper name is called a ....

14 A link which represents a class which is not strictly superordinate to a previous link is called a ....

15 The zero indicator symbol for form divisions is a ....

16 An .... link is one which represents a concept for which readers are unlikely to search when looking for the specific subject represented by the final digit of the class number.

17 A heading may be inverted when its .... class is not represented in the chain.

18 Form divisions require a .... in the index.

19 Digits added to a schedule number as the result of a ' divide like ' note are: a) ignored; b) treated in a special manner; c) treated in the same way as any other digit.

20 Area subdivisions are/are not analysed and indexed in the same way as the rest of a class number.

ANSWERS

APPENDIX III

Although this text has been concerned specifically with the decimal classification scheme, edition 17, it must be pointed out that the technique works with other systems. Note, however, that great care must be exercised with those schemes which do not reveal their hierarchical structure in the notation.

Universal Decimal Classification Scheme

Analysis of polymers by gas chromatography   541.64 : 543.544

541.64.543.544	—Gas chromatography
541.64 : 543.54	—Adsorption methods
541.64 : 543.5	—Physical chemical methods Unsought link
541.64 : 543	—Analytical chemistry
541.64	—Polymers
541.64	—Macromolecular chemistry
541.6	—Chemical structure in relation to properties Unsought link
541	—General, theoretical and physical chemistry
54	—Chemistry
5	—Mathematical and natural sciences

Index entries:

GAS CHROMATOGRAPHY: Analytical chemistry: Polymers— 541.64 : 543.544

CHROMOTOGRAPHY: Analytical chemistry: Polymers—541.64 : 543.544

ADSORPTION METHODS: Analytical chemistry: Polymers— 541.64 : 543.54

ANALYTICAL CHEMISTRY: Polymers—541.64 : 543

POLYMERS: Chemistry—541.64

MACROMOLECULAR CHEMISTRY—541.64

PHYSICAL CHEMISTRY—541

CHEMISTRY—54

SCIENCE—5

NATURAL SCIENCE—5

Library of Congress
An introduction to vector analysis   QA261
QA261—Vector analysis
QA251—Universal algebra. Linear algebra
QA152/297—Algebra
QA—Mathematics
Q—Science
Index entries:
VECTOR ANALYSIS: Algebra—QA261
LINEAR ALGEBRA—QA251/263
ALGEBRA—QA152/297
MATHEMATICS—QA
SCIENCE—Q
NATURAL SCIENCES—Q

Communism in the United States   HX653
HX653—United States
HX651/780—By country   Unsought link
HX626/999—Communism
Index entries:
USA: Communism—HX653
COMMUNISM—HX626/999

Prison visiting: a social worker's guide   HV7428
HV7428—Social work with delinquents and criminals
HV7231/9920—Penology
HV6001/9920—Criminology
HV—Social pathology
Index entries:
PRISON VISITING: Penology—HV7428
SOCIAL WORK: Criminals: Penology—HV7428
SOCIAL WORK: Delinquents: Penology—HV7428
PENOLOGY—HV7231/9920
CRIMINOLOGY—HV6001/9920
SOCIAL PATHOLOGY—HV
PATHOLOGY, SOCIAL—HV

Bibliographic Classification
Electrodynamics of planetary bodies   DF,O

DF,O—Electrodynamics
DF—Planets, the solar system
D/DF—Astronomy
A/G—Science. Natural sciences
Index entries:
ELECTRODYNAMICS: Planets—DF,O
PLANETS: Astronomy—DF
ASTRONOMY—D/DF
SCIENCE—A/G
NATURAL STUDIES—A/G

Medieval castles in Northumberland: an architectural guide VCP,Bern
VCP,Bern —Northumberland
VCP,Ber —Northeastern England   Unsought link
VCP,Be —Great Britain
VCP,B —Medieval
VCP —Palaces, castles, chateau, etc
VCN/VCP —Architecture of dwellings
VCE/VCY —Practical architecture
VC —Art, technic, education and profession of architecture
                Unsought link
VA/VD —Architecture
Index entries:
NORTHUMBERLAND: Medieval castles: Architecture—VCP,Bern
GREAT BRITAIN: Medieval castles: Architecture—VCP,Be
MEDIEVAL CASTLES: Architecture—VCP,B
CASTLES: Architecture—VCP
DWELLINGS: Architecture—VCN/VCP
ARCHITECTURE—VA/VD

Mail order marketing   TJUQ
TJUQ—Mail order retailing
TJU —Retail mercantile business
TJQ/TJY—Mercantile business   Unsought link
TJ —Business
T —Economics
Index entries:
MAIL ORDER: Retail business—TJUQ
RETAIL BUSINESS—TJU
BUSINESS—TJ
ECONOMICS—T

APPENDIX IV

BIBLIOGRAPHY

COATES, E J: *Subject catalogues: headings and structure.* Library Association, 1960. Chapters IX and X.

MILLS, J: *Chain indexing and the classified catalogue.* Library Association Record 57, 1955, 141-148.

RANGANATHAN, S R: 'Chain procedure: its development, its uses, its light on basic class and its problems.' DRTC Seminar no 3, 1965, paper U.

RANGANATHAN, S R: *Classified catalogue code.* Asia Publishing House, 5th edition 1964. Chapters KB and KC.

TOPIC INDEX

This index is provided to help you to revise specific points about chain indexing once you have worked through the full text. The frame number given is that in which the topic is first introduced.